YOU MUST REMEMBER THIS

1955

MILESTONES, MEMORIES,
TRIVIA AND FACTS, NEWS EVENTS,
PROMINENT PERSONALITIES &
SPORTS HIGHLIGHTS OF THE YEAR

TO : _____

FROM : _____

MESSAGE : _____

_____

selected and researched
by
mary a. pradt

WARNER **W** TREASURES ™

PUBLISHED BY WARNER BOOKS

A TIME WARNER COMPANY

Warner Books, Inc.
1271 Avenue of the Americas
New York, New York 10020

Warner Treasures is a
trademark of Warner Books, Inc.

 A Time Warner Company

DESIGN:
CAROL BOKUNIEWICZ DESIGN
PRINTED IN SINGAPORE
FIRST PRINTING : MAY 1995
10 9 8 7 6 5 4 3 2 1
ISBN: 0-446-91031-7

Led by the
reverend martin luther king, jr.
Blacks and others launched a boycott of the segregated bus system in Montgomery, Alabama.

Physicist and humanist Albert Einstein died in Princeton, NJ, in April, at age 76. Driven from Germany by the Nazis, he convinced the U.S. to develop the nuclear bomb. Later, he urged the bomb never be used.

MILLIONS OF KIDS LINED UP FOR THE POLIO VACCINE DEVELOPED BY DR. JONAS SALK, EFFECTIVELY ENDING A DECADE OF EPIDEMIC POLIO

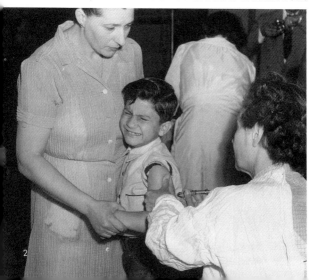

President Dwight D. Eisenhower suffered a heart attack September 24, 1955. Eisenhower (1890-1969) would go on to serve another term. His VP for both terms, of course, was

richard nixon

newsreel

Look more closely at the year 1955, and you can spot many events and trends that would dominate news and culture for much of the twentieth century.

SIR WINSTON CHURCHILL RETIRED AT AGE 80 AND STEPPED DOWN AS BRITISH PRIME MINISTER.

international

headlines

The Warsaw Pact formed in May 1955. The Communist version of NATO, the pact included the Soviet Union, Poland, Czechoslovakia, Hungary, Romania, Bulgaria, Albania, and East Germany.

In Argentina, Juan Peron was ousted as president and exiled, after a decade of power. When his downfall came, crowds thronged the city streets, some dragging statues of Peron's late wife, Eva ("Evita").

SAIGON AND THE GAZA STRIP WERE HEATING UP WITH FACTIONAL FIGHTING.

The Big Four Summit in Geneva, with Britain, the U.S., France, and the Soviet Union represented, claimed itself a success, even though no firm agreements were reached on German issues or disarmament.

DISNEYLAND OPENED IN ANAHEIM, CA. THE
244-ACRE PARK COST $17 MILLION TO BUILD AND
DEFINED THE IDEA OF THE THEME PARK. THE
DISNEY EMPIRE EXTENDED FAR BEYOND
ANAHEIM. "DISNEYLAND" WAS THE 4TH-RANKING
PRIME-TIME TV SERIES IN THE 1955-56 SEASON.
ON AFTERSCHOOL TV, THE "MICKEY MOUSE CLUB"
PREMIERED IN 1955.

POLYESTER

IN JANUARY 1955, DuPont debuted its first no-iron Dacron fiber, "Fantastique." You can't overestimate the impact that wash-and-wear,

IS BORN!

quick-dry fabrics would have on our clothes and our lifestyle.

THE U.S. MINIMUM WAGE WAS RAISED BY EISENHOWER TO $1 AN HOUR.

cultural
milestones

Coonskin caps were the only acceptable headwear (other than Mousketeer ears) for a young American in 1955. "The Adventures of Davy Crockett," also on early-evening TV, launched this instant craze.

GENERAL MOTORS BECAME THE FIRST CORPORATION TO EARN MORE THAN $1 BILLION IN A SINGLE YEAR.

7

television

ANOTHER GROUNDBREAKING
KIDDIE SHOW PREMIERED IN
OCTOBER 1955—"CAPTAIN
KANGAROO," WHICH BECAME THE
LONGEST-RUNNING CHILDREN'S
PROGRAM IN TELEVISION HISTORY.

By 1955, almost two-thirds of American homes had TV; phenomenal, considering that in 1950, only 9 percent of Americans had sets. Television was beginning to transform our personal and political landscape. Who could predict such lofty impact, when the top-rated shows for the 1955-56 fall season were:

1. "The $64,000 Question" (CBS)

2. "I Love Lucy" (CBS)

3. "The Ed Sullivan Show" (CBS)

4. "Disneyland" (ABC)

5. "The Jack Benny Show" (CBS)

6. "December Bride" (CBS)

7. "You Bet Your Life" (NBC)

8. "Dragnet" (NBC)

9. "The Millionaire" (CBS)

10. "I've Got a Secret" (CBS)

11. "General Electric Theater" (CBS)

12. "Private Secretary" (CBS)

13. "Ford Theater" (NBC)

14. "The Red Skelton Show" (CBS)

15. "The George Gobel Show" (NBC)

"the $64,000 question"

hosted by Hal March, was enormously popular, but short-lived (1955-59). Its downfall was the biggest of the TV quiz-show scandals. Many of the contestants, in their supposedly hermeticallysealed isolation booths, were actually fed the answers.

Actress Debbie Reynolds married crooner Eddie Fisher in New York, September 26, 1955. Each would go on to other liaisons, Eddie most notably with Elizabeth Taylor.

celeb wedding of the year

milestones

royal wedding of the year

Italian princess Maria Pia, 20, eldest daughter of ex-King Umberto of Italy, married Prince Alexander of Yugoslavia, 30, son of ex-Regent Prince Paul and cousin of exiled King Peter. Guests included most of Europe's one-time and would-be kings and queens, about 100 princes and princesses, and dozens of dukes and duchesses.

DEATHS

James Dean
died September 30, 1955, at 24, after crashing his Porsche coupe on the road between L.A. and Salinas, en route to an auto rally. His cult following persists to this day. *Rebel Without a Cause* was his only film released before his death; *East of Eden* and *Giant* were shown posthumously.

Charlie "Bird" Parker,
saxophone great and seminal figure in "Bebop" jazz, died at 34, after a long struggle with drug abuse and mental problems.

Dale Carnegie,
author of *How to Win Friends and Influence People*, an enormously successful self-help book first published in 1936, died November 1, 1955, at 64.

Walter White,
head of the NAACP, died at 61. Although White had only a small proportion of African ancestry and could have "passed" for Caucasian, he chose to identify himself as Negro and fought a lifelong campaign against racism.

Cy Young
the famous pitcher who had a record 511 wins, died November 4, 1955.

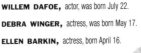

show biz births

KEVIN COSTNER, actor, was born January 18.

ARSENIO HALL, comedian/talk show host, February 12.

MARGAUX HEMINGWAY, model, born February 19.

BO DEREK, actress, was born November 20.

DAVID LEE ROTH, October 10 — singer/songwriter.

BRUCE WILLIS, actor, March 19.

JOHN TRAVOLTA, actor, February 18.

WILLEM DAFOE, actor, was born July 22.

DEBRA WINGER, actress, was born May 17.

ELLEN BARKIN, actress, born April 16.

11

1 **cherry pink and apple blossom white** recorded by Perez ('King of the Mambo') Prado and his orchestra, was the number one hit of 1955.

2 **sincerely** The McGuire Sisters

3 **rock around the clock** Bill Haley and the Comets. The song has been featured in at least 14 films and has been recorded in 35 different languages.

4 **sixteen tons** recorded by Tennessee Ernie Ford

5 **love is a many-splendored thing** by the Four Aces. This song was the Academy Award winner.

6 **the yellow rose of texas** Mitch Miller

7 **the ballad of davy crockett** The theme song of the TV series, this was Bill Hayes's only million-seller. Fess Parker, the star of the TV show, also recorded the theme song of the legendary "king of the wild frontier."

'55

hit music

8 **autumn leaves** Roger Williams, pianist. Nat "King" Cole also sang it in the film *Autumn Leaves*.

9 **let me go, lover** Joan Weber, age 18, recorded this song and gained her only gold record with it.

10 **dance with me, henry** Georgia Gibbs. Hank Ballard had recorded this as "Work with Me, Annie," but it was considered too suggestive. Georgia Gibbs's cover version cleaned up the lyrics and sold a million copies.

ROCK around the clock

Simulated Stereo

DECCA

BILL HALEY COMETS

13

fiction

1. **marjorie morningstar**
   herman wouk

2. **auntie mame**
   patrick dennis

3. **andersonville**
   mackinlay kantor

4. **bonjour tristesse**
   francoise sagan

5. **the man in the gray flannel suit**
   sloan wilson

6. **something of value**
   robert ruark

7. **not as a stranger**
   morton thompson

8. **no time for sergeants**
   mac hyman

9. **the tontine**
   thomas b. costain

10. **ten north frederick**
    john o'hara

other important books

NOTES OF A NATIVE SON JAMES BALDWIN

LORD OF THE RINGS J.R.R. TOLKIEN

LOLITA VLADIMIR NABOKOV

ELOISE KAY THOMPSON. The illustrated story of a six-year-old girl who lives at the Plaza Hotel in New York. "I am a city child," says Eloise.

bestselling

nonfiction **books**

1. **the gift from the sea**
   anne morrow lindbergh

2. **the power of positive thinking**
   norman vincent peale

3. **the family of man**
   edward steichen

4. **a man called peter**
   catherine marshall

5. **how to live 365 days a year**
   john a. schindler

6. **better homes and garden diet book**

7. **the secret of happiness**
   billy graham

8. **why johnny can't read**
   rudolph flesch

9. **inside africa**
   john gunther

10. **year of decisions**
    harry s truman

15

BOXING

Boxing was hugely popular in the mid-fifties. In 1955, Sugar Ray Robinson came out of retirement at 35 to regain the middleweight title, knocking out Carl Olson. Unbeaten Rocky Marciano, the heavyweight, KO'd Archie Moore in the fifth round to retain his title.

AT THE INDIANAPOLIS 500, BILL VUKOVICH, TRYING FOR AN UNPARALLELED THIRD CONSECUTIVE VICTORY, DIED WHEN, AT A SPEED OVER 100 MPH, HE PLOWED INTO A PILEUP CAUSED BY EXTREME WINDS.

IN MAY 1955, WILT CHAMBERLAIN, 7'2", ANNOUNCED HE WOULD ATTEND THE UNIVERSITY OF KANSAS.

THE CLEVELAND BROWNS DEFEATED THE LOS ANGELES RAMS FOR THE NATIONAL FOOTBALL LEAGUE CHAMPIONSHIP, 38-14. IN PASADENA, OHIO STATE DEFEATED SOUTHERN CAL 20-7 IN THE ROSE BOWL.

sports

The Brooklyn Dodgers won their first World Series October 5, 1955. "Dem Bums," as they were affectionately known, had previously lost the Series eight times, the last five times to the Yankees, or Bronx Bombers. The Dodgers took the Series four games to three on a final shutout pitched by Johnny Podres. In the game's fourth inning, Roy Campanella went home on a single by Gil Hodges, who also sent Pee Wee Reese home in the sixth inning. Campanella was named National League MVP. The 1955 series remains legendary both in Brooklyn and in baseball history.

Marty was the year's most honored movie, when the Academy Awards for 1955 were handed out March 21, 1956. It took Best Picture honors over *Love Is a Many-Splendored Thing*, *Mister Roberts*, *Picnic*, and *The Rose Tattoo*. **Ernest Borgnine** won Best Actor Oscar for *Marty*, winning out over James Cagney, James Dean, Frank Sinatra, and Spencer Tracy. **Delbert Mann**, director of *Marty*, won Best Directing Oscar over Joshua Logan, John Sturges, David Lean, and Elia Kazan. **Paddy Chayefsky** won for *Marty's* screenplay. **Anna Magnani** won the Academy Award for Best Actress in *The Rose Tattoo*.

rebel without a cause
established the cult of James Dean. Dean was posthumously nominated for the Best Actor Oscar for *East of Eden*, but lost to Ernest Borgnine.

THEATER IN 1955 TENNESSEE WILLIAMS'S *CAT ON A HOT TIN ROOF* WAS THE SEASON'S MOST IMPORTANT PLAY. *DAMN YANKEES* WAS THE TOP NEW MUSICAL.

the seven-year itch
CONTINUED TO BUILD
UP MARILYN MONROE'S
SUPERSTAR STATUS

movies

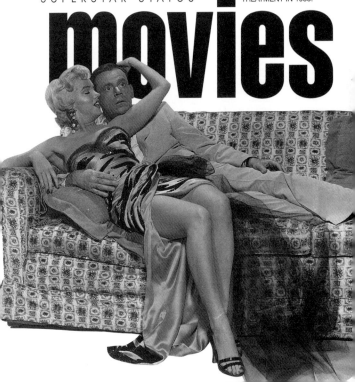

55 "The stodgy car died in 1955"

"The stodgy car died in 1955," wrote an auto historian. The 1955 Chevy is regarded as Chevrolet's finest hour. This was the

cars

year Detroit began "a six-6 dive into Hedonism." It had a new V-8 engine and low-slung flashy styling.

For budget-minded young people

(from 16 to 66)

The Ford Mainline Tudor shown here is the lowest priced sedan with proved V-8 power that you can buy. Yet, like all the '55 Fords, it brings you new Thunderbird-inspired styling...*roomier*, more colorful Luxury Lounge interiors...a wrap-around windshield...a smoother Angle-Poised ride...and Trigger-Torque power that obeys your commands quicker than you can wink!

The 6-passenger Country Sedan—like all Ford wagons—does double duty on a single-car budget. Ford's station wagon choice includes 2-doors, 4-doors, seats for 6 or 8.

The Fairlane Victoria is America's most beautiful buy. It has the "open" style of a convertible, the snug comfort of a smart sedan. It's one of six new Ford Fairlane models.

The Customline Fordor is another of Ford's budget-priced family favorites. And you can have power steering, brakes, windows and 4-way power seat—all at moderate extra cost.

Ford Try a Trigger-Torque "Take-Off"!

PRT, June 1955 (Adv)

fashion

the new easy-care

synthetics worked well in shirtlike blouses and shirt-waist dresses with full skirts. Several nylon "crinolines" gave you that extra fullness. You soaked them in sugar and let dry for extra bouf-fancy. A cinch belt could accentuate the waistline. High fashion leaned more to pencil-slim sheath dresses and skirts. Givenchy's long, slim 1955 sheath, about three inches below the knees, was accessorized, of course, with hat and gloves.

for men, 1955 was the year of the Man
in the Gray Flannel Suit, both in the Sloan Wilson novel of that name and in real life. Of course, 1955 was also the beginning of the rebellious youth fashion trend, exemplified by James Dean's and Brando's studied "look"—tight black T-shirt, jeans, black leather jacket, and cowboy boots.

final factoid

**Selchow &
Righter
introduce
the
game
of
Scrabble**

archive photos: inside front cover, pages 1, 5, 11, 13, 15, 16, 22, inside back cover.

associated press: pages 2, 4, 10.

photofest: pages 3, 4, 6, 8, 9, 18, 19.

original photography:
beth phillips: pages 13, 14, 21, 25.

album cover:
courtesy of bob george/
the archive of contemporary music: page 13

book cover:
courtesy of jessy randell and glenn horowitz: page 14

design:
carol bokuniewicz design

'5.5